BIG AL'S MLM
SPONSORING
MAGIC

HOW TO BUILD A NETWORK MARKETING TEAM QUICKLY

BY TOM "BIG AL" SCHREITER

For information, contact:

Fortune Network Publishing
PO Box 890084
Houston, TX 77289 USA
Telephone: +1 (281) 280-9800

ISBN: 1-892366-13-4

ISBN-13: 978-1-892366-13-9

DEDICATION

This book is dedicated to network marketers everywhere.

I travel the world 240+ days each year. Let me know if you want me to stop in your area and conduct a live Big Al training.

http://www.BigAlSeminars.com

Get 7 mini-reports of amazing, easy sentences that create new, hot prospects.

Sign up today at:
http://www.BigAlReport.com

Other great Big Al Books available at:
http://www.BigAlBooks.com

Table of Contents

PREFACE

Ready to do your network marketing business as a business? Don't have time for trial and error? In a hurry to build a solid group and then grow from there?

Network marketing isn't measured in clicks and "Likes" … it is a people business. Products and services don't have legs. People move products and services, and you are now in the people business. Discover how to move people and you will succeed.

Focus on the basic step-by-step system in this book, and get ready for a fun and exciting business. Every business is easier with a roadmap.

Experience the business through the eyes of Distributor Joe, and you can relate to the lessons without the rejection and frustrations of trial and error. Let "Big Al" be your guide through the hundreds of questions on starting your business.

Now you have a proven guide for your new and growing organization of distributors.

-- Tom "Big Al" Schreiter

Distributor Joe

Distributor Joe wakes up early on Saturday morning. All week he looked forward to his day off to do some "real recruiting." No job to interfere today, just 100% effort to sponsor distributors.

After finishing a hearty breakfast, Joe looked at the clock. 8:30 a.m. - time to make those telephone appointments.

A little hesitant, Joe dials the first number. The telephone rings three times and Joe quickly hangs up. "They might still be in bed. I guess I shouldn't be calling this early," Joe thinks to himself. "I should do some goal-setting for an hour."

At 9:30 a.m., Joe finishes his revised goal and projections chart showing how much bonus he will receive if each of his tenth-level distributors sponsors just one person a week who averages $20.30 in weekly volume. He has also calculated the number of personal speaking engagements he can fit into his schedule when he reaches superstar status.

But first, Joe has to sponsor that **first distributor**.

At 9:35 a.m., Joe makes his second phone call. The line is busy. With a feeling of relief, Joe thinks, "He probably wouldn't be interested anyway."

Time to check Facebook messages. Maybe someone lost their job and might message Joe, asking for an opportunity.

No luck.

Since Joe failed to get an appointment with his first two prospects, he decides to research his prospect list to see who else he can contact.

While researching his Facebook Friends list, Joe notices that it is already time for a coffee break. Good time to read today's newspaper. After all, it's Saturday.

Maybe during his coffee break, Joe could come up with a great idea for a picture to post on the Internet. Yeah, that's a good plan.

After coffee, it's back to work. Joe researches which pictures on the Internet get the most comments. Might as well make sure that his picture will be a success.

Before Joe decides on a picture, it is time for the weekly conference call. Can't make telephone appointments now. Time to listen to the upline leaders who earn big bonus checks, probably because they talk to many "live" prospects every day. And another hour passes by.

"Wow! That was a great call," Joe says to himself. "It is almost noon now. People will be eating. Maybe I should just listen to some pre-recorded calls from previous weeks."

At 1:00 p.m., Joe begins to feel a little guilty that he has done everything except recruiting this morning. He thinks to himself, "I'm not really afraid to talk to people or get rejections. I'm just setting a good foundation for a big afternoon. As a matter of fact, I'm ready to go out now and recruit in a big way."

As Joe gets ready to leave the house, he suddenly comes to his senses and remarks, "Whoops, I forgot about my lunch. I'd better eat before I leave."

At 2:00 p.m., Joe finally leaves his house and pulls out of the driveway. But where should he go first? No appointments. No plans.

Joe gets up his courage and heads for the little neighborhood shopping district to make some cold calls. His opportunity is good and these are small business people he is going to call on … should be a perfect match for success.

The donut shop owner had a line of customers in his shop, so Joe wisely passed him by.

The office supply store owner had only one person inside, but if Joe got rejected, that customer might think poorly of Joe and his opportunity.

The flower shop lady had a sour face. Best not stop in and make her more upset.

At the shoe store, only a young salesperson was on the floor. However, if Joe presented his opportunity to the salesperson, Joe might be caught by the manager of the store and thrown out.

Ah, but the watch repair shop owner was alone.

Joe introduced himself. The watch repair shop owner immediately took control by asking, "How much money is this going to cost me? How long have you been doing this? What are your credentials? Can you show me your last 12 bonus checks?"

Totally intimidated, Joe saved face by saying he was very busy and had another appointment, and he quickly left.

At 3:20 p.m. Joe entered his car, quite discouraged. He realized his self-confidence was at zero, but he wanted to make one more effort. Joe decided to drive by his friend's house and make at least one presentation.

At 3:45 p.m., Joe drove down the street in front of his friend's house, careful not to enter the driveway. From the street, Joe could see no activity through the front window. Since it appeared that no one was home, Joe said to himself,

"Well, now is probably a good time to head home and check my email messages. A successful businessman must communicate promptly."

"Big Al" ... A Clue to Success

Distributor Joe had a professional sponsor named **Big Al**. When Big Al called Joe to see how Saturday went, he already knew what Joe would report.

He said, "Joe, I know you were eager to do well, and I know that insecure feeling that creeps over all of us when we recruit. I think after that experience you may be willing to listen to my advice on how to cure that problem **permanently**."

Joe's spirits immediately lifted as he hurried to Big Al's house to learn the secret solution to his recruiting problem.

When Joe arrived, Big Al said,

"One lesson is worth 10,000 words. Most distributors get good advice but never realize the value or put it to use. I am not going to tell you the magic solution to your recruiting problem. You'll learn that for yourself.

"For now, here is what I would like you to do. Of all of the people you know, friends, relatives, co-workers, are there at least a few people who **feel** the same way you do? You know, maybe they want more money or a career where they have more time?"

Distributor Joe thought for a moment and said, "Yes. I know a couple of people who **feel** the same way I do."

Big Al then said, "Make a few phone calls and set some appointments for Tuesday night. Don't worry about anything as I will go with you and I will do all the talking. You'll just tag along and watch, okay?"

"What should I say?" asked Distributor Joe.

Big Al continued. "These are your close friends. You don't need a sales script. Just say what comes to you naturally such as, 'Are you interested in some extra money? I want you to meet this guy, Big Al. Let's get together at your house Tuesday night for 20 minutes. You'll just love meeting him.'"

Joe felt this was not too hard. After all, he didn't have to do anything but set an appointment. The whole presentation would be done by Big Al. Joe could just sit back, let his friends blast away with all kinds of questions and objections, and watch Big Al handle them and make them distributors.

Big Al pointed to the telephone and said, "Why not make a call or two now?"

Joe was motivated. In just 20 minutes he had set up four appointments for Tuesday night. And handling questions on the phone was a breeze since Joe's attitude was super-positive.

When asked, "What's it all about?" Joe would reply, "I just want you to meet Big Al, he's got a lot of ideas on making money and you'll think he's a pretty neat guy."

Big Al turned to Joe and said, "Go home and relax. We'll meet at your house on Tuesday night at 5:30 p.m. after you get off work. You have already accomplished more in 20 minutes than most distributors do in a week."

Two Against One:
The Unfair Advantage

Tuesday night went so smoothly that Joe was at a loss for words. One appointment wasn't interested, one appointment had to think it over, and **two appointments became distributors**. Imagine, two brand new first-level distributors in just one evening!

And it was easy. Joe just introduced Big Al to his prospect and Big Al calmly showed the opportunity. When Big Al was done, the prospect either joined or not. There was no magical presentation, no high pressure, just a simple explanation that Joe could probably do just as well.

But what was amazing was how the prospects reacted. They listened to every word Big Al said. They treated him with respect. There were no cynical objections. The prospects were on their best behavior. That made Big Al's job easy.

When Big Al and Joe arrived back at Joe's house later that evening, Joe asked Big Al to come inside to explain the wonderful happenings of that evening. Big Al smiled and told Joe to begin taking notes.

Big Al said, "The secret of recruiting this evening was simple. **There were two of us and only one of them**. They were at an unfair advantage. All we had to do was convince one person to our way of thinking. And our thinking must have some merit, because there are two of us who already share it. It is easier for the prospect to join our enthusiasm than it is for the prospect to convince two of us that we're wrong. Besides, your prospect wants to think like we do. He wants extra money, too."

Big Al continued. "This may seem simple, but most professional recruiters work in pairs. Knowing this secret is vital to your success. Let's take a closer look at **why** professionals work in pairs."

1. When you visit a friend he may sidetrack you with stories, sports talk, and chatter about your families. He can joke with you, tease you, and give you all kinds of grief just for the fun of it.

   But the scene changes drastically when you are with a stranger. He is polite since he doesn't know me. He feels I'm an expert because I'm a stranger. I may be your boss, so he is on his best behavior not to embarrass you. He may feel he can intimidate you, but with a stranger along, he will be cooperative and business-like.

2. Your prospect sees only you, not the company you represent. If he feels you are in some way inadequate personally, he will reject the opportunity based on you, not the company. However, if a stranger is along whom he doesn't know personally, he must make a decision on the facts at hand, not on you and your present position.

3. When two people work as a team, their self-confidence is at a high level. They keep each other motivated. It's not like taking on the world alone. If you are by yourself, you are probably afraid of rejection, afraid to make appointments, and more likely to avoid contact with prospects.

   That's why you spent Saturday doing paperwork. If you had a companion, each would work hard not to let the other one down. If each were to make four appointments, you'd be sure to keep up your end of the load. Neither person wants to be the first one to quit.

4. When two distributors make a presentation, one talks, the other keeps quiet and observes. The observer does not have to worry about making sure the presentation has all the information in order, etc., so he is free to closely observe the prospect and listen for clues to his motivation. When it comes time for the prospect to make a decision, the observer may be able to help with some vital information that otherwise might be overlooked.

5. Two distributors working together accomplish more than each working separately. I'm sure you now see why you are much more efficient working as a team. Professionals look for efficiency.

6. If you do not work as a team and have your new distributors recruit alone, you are then assuming the following:

   (a) Your new distributors have instant and complete knowledge of your business.

   (b) Your new distributors are blessed with unlimited self-confidence and can handle rejection alone.

   (c) Your new distributors became instantly competent to present the opportunity by virtue of filling out their distributor applications.

   To assume the above would be ridiculous. Therefore, the only alternative is to work as a team.

7. When two distributors work together, there is an opportunity to evaluate each presentation. They can review the good points and the not-so-good points of the previous presentation to make sure their next presentation will be even better. Having two separate viewpoints, the presenter and the observer, is invaluable.

"As you can see, Joe, common sense dictates that recruiting should be done in pairs. For the next two weeks, you and I will work together Tuesday nights and Saturdays. We'll need four appointments each Tuesday and six appointments on Saturdays. That's ten a week. I'll make five appointments and you make five. Fair enough?"

Joe enthusiastically agreed. This was going to be easy. All of his fears about recruiting were gone and Joe saw a bright future with lots of distributors.

I Can't Believe It Was So Easy

"So why was this so easy?" asked Distributor Joe. "It was so easy to get an appointment. It was so easy to sit down with my friends. It was so easy to sign up new distributors. What's going on?"

Big Al replied, "Well, it wasn't the presentation that did the work. You noticed that my presentation was simply giving a few facts and then asking what else they wanted to know. So let me tell you the inside secret to all of this."

Distributor Joe was ready to learn, so Big Al continued.

"People make a decision to join your business **before** you even start your presentation. The presentation had nothing to do with it. Your friend made an instant decision to set the appointment before the presentation. Your friend wanted to join or else your friend wouldn't even let us come by and visit."

Distributor Joe's eyes got wide. "Wow! That's incredible. So are you telling me that my prospects have already made a 'Yes' decision **before** I have started my presentation?"

"You got it!" said Big Al. "Later, after we cover some more basics with you, you will learn the closing skills. Out of the 25 skills in network marketing, closing is one of the most important skills. But for now, consider this.

"A woman walks into a shoe store and sees 1,000 shoes on display. How long does it take her to make a decision on each individual pair of shoes? Micro-seconds! She immediately makes a decision on style and color, using internal programs that tell her what she likes. This is all before there is a presentation about the quality of the shoe, where it was made, etc.

"A man goes to a football game. He has already made a decision about who he wants to win, even before the game has started. He has internal programs that tell him what he likes.

"When you called your friend and asked if he wanted to earn some extra money, your friend had an internal program that already told him that he wanted to move forward in life instead of staying where he was. That is why he made a decision to set the appointment.

"Humans make quick decisions. We need to manage those quick decisions. In the system I have shown you so far, the system makes handling this easy. And like I said, you don't have to learn everything your first month. I will teach you the 25 basic skills one by one. But for now, just use this simple system while you learn."

Distributor Joe thought about this for a moment. Yes, people do seem to make up their minds quickly, so the presentation isn't the issue. It is what happens first that makes the difference.

So why not follow this system with Big Al for a while and see what happens?

The Payoff

After two weeks Joe had 15 distributors in his group. It was almost becoming routine. On Tuesday evenings and Saturdays, Big Al and Joe would present the opportunity and let the prospects decide if they wanted to join. No magic, no high pressure. Just show the opportunity.

Big Al and Joe were having coffee when Big Al announced, "Joe, your training is done. You are on your own now. You have heard my presentation so many times, you can say it better than I can."

Joe looked bewildered, "But we are a team, aren't we?"

Big Al laughed and said, "Joe, I don't want you to go out and recruit alone, I want you to team up with your new distributors. Sure, you and I can eventually sponsor 1,000 distributors ourselves, but that's not how network marketing works. You've got to work smart, not hard.

"You have to train your distributors just like I trained you. Wouldn't you rather have five or ten of your new distributors out recruiting, instead of you doing it all? Don't you think your new distributors will get discouraged unless you work with them as a team? Besides, Joe, you are going to run out of friends to talk to.

"Instead of making cold calls, running ads, etc., doesn't it make more sense to be talking to friends? You have 15 new distributors, some motivated, some not. Ask them to set appointments just like I asked you. You'll probably have at least four or five distributors who are serious about the opportunity and they will want you to work with them.

Working with those four or five serious distributors will keep you busy for a long, long time.

"You'll then have a large, strong, and deep organization of distributors. This is the fastest and surest way of becoming a superstar in network marketing."

Joe did some quick mental calculations. If he could work with just five of his new distributors so they would each have 15 distributors, that would be 75 new distributors in his group! Plus, he would now have five fully-trained distributors who could work with their distributors. That could be hundreds more distributors in his group. Joe was beginning to understand the word "efficiency."

Instead of each distributor floundering about on his own, by using teamwork, Joe could have hundreds of distributors in his organization in just two or three months. Big Al spent three weeks training Joe, so it would only take Joe two or three months to train his four or five key distributors by working with them two at a time. Joe could work with one distributor on Tuesdays and Saturdays and a different distributor on Wednesdays and Thursdays.

Just think, in 60 to 90 days, Joe would have a group that would be the envy of his peers. All Joe had to do was follow The System.

Big Al pointed out to Joe that he could become a superstar just by using the basics he had learned in the last three weeks. However, Big Al insisted that he and Joe meet weekly to keep Joe on course and to improve Joe's recruiting skills.

Joe then thanked Big Al for all the help, not realizing that Big Al had just added another strong downline group of distributors through Joe.

Not Everyone Is A Worker

Two weeks later, while having coffee, Distributor Joe and Big Al discussed the wisdom of The System. Distributor Joe realized that sponsoring too many new distributors personally would be senseless. Because if Joe had to work with too many new distributors, then Joe's original distributors would quit because of lack of training and attention.

Distributor Joe asked, "It makes sense to limit the number of personally enrolled distributors. But what if only two or three of the original 15 distributors were serious workers? What about the other unmotivated distributors? Did we make a mistake in sponsoring unmotivated distributors?"

Big Al answered, "It is well known that unmotivated distributors use the product and can be good wholesale customers. You may have hundreds of dollars of volume monthly just servicing your unmotivated distributors. Certainly we should help them and not ignore them.

"Unmotivated distributors have different goals than you, Joe. They may have joined only to sell and make a few extra dollars, or they just wanted to buy wholesale for themselves, or they just enjoyed being involved with your community of positive distributors. My personal organization does several thousand dollars monthly of 'internal consumption.'

"The problem here, Joe, is that you are missing the big picture. You did not sponsor an unmotivated distributor, you sponsored **a valuable contact who knows dozens of good quality prospects, who when sponsored, will become workers**. In other words, don't judge the unmotivated distributor for what he might do. Judge him for the potential distributors in his organization.

"Your job is to work in depth by getting referrals from your unmotivated distributor. Surely he knows at least one person who can become a good worker in your organization.

"Professional recruiters readily admit that they probably didn't sponsor most of their workers. Their workers were probably second level, third level, or even 10th level distributors who, like cream, rose to the top.

"Never hesitate to sponsor an unmotivated distributor. His personal goals may change and he could develop into a worker, or he may lead you to a worker you would have never met."

Myth-Killing

The following week at their regular coffee meeting, Joe confessed to being tempted to do some exciting innovations in recruiting. Joe had researched some good ideas and wanted to know if he could implement these for faster growth.

Not that The System wasn't working. As a matter of fact, Joe now had over 85 distributors in his organization after only seven weeks in the business. It was just that these new ideas sounded so fabulous, and Joe just couldn't wait to try them out.

Big Al smiled and took a deep breath. "Joe, I guess it's time to do some myth-killing. Every distributor has his pet idea on how to recruit fast. Some may work partially, some may only collect applications, some can be used only by people with special talents, and some only work in unusual circumstances. The reason pros use The System is because it works. Anyone can use it and leap to the top in a matter of weeks.

"The reason I insisted on meeting weekly was to keep you on track, Joe. Following various recruiting ideas in a scattered manner will only bog you down and take away time from The System. If you are busy writing advertising, then your new distributor is sitting home alone and nothing is happening. Keep on The System and avoid being swayed from your present course. But I don't want you to take my word on it.

"Let's examine together some of the major recruiting myths and analyze their weaknesses. With this knowledge, we won't be tempted to stray from our proven course."

The next three hours were spent analyzing why many of the other recruiting methods do not work consistently for most beginning distributors. Here are some of the major myths and their weaknesses:

1. **Newspaper and Internet Ads — Help Wanted.** Imagine an unemployed 17-year-old reading the paper. No money, no car, just looking for a few dollars for his next date. The problem with Help Wanted Ads is that you reach the unemployed who need money now. They can't wait several months to build a business. They want to know how much salary the job pays. The real people you want are those with jobs who want to build a part-time business. Since they don't read the Help Wanted ads, why advertise there?

2. **Newspaper and Internet Ads — Business Opportunity.** While the readership is smaller, you do reach business people looking to buy a business. They probably have accumulated enough cash to hire a manager to run their network marketing business for them.

    But is network marketing a business you can buy? No, it is a business that requires personal effort. Obviously this is not the best place to find workers willing to go out and start a business.

3. **Unemployment Office.** The majority of the people at the office fall into two categories:

    (a) Those who do not wish to look for a job and just want to collect unemployment. We certainly wouldn't want to upset these people by giving them an opportunity to work.

    (b) Those looking for work who have been unable to find a job. These people need a job now, not a business opportunity that will pay off in the months ahead. (See #1.)

4.   **Employment Agencies** — See #1.

5.   **Door-to-Door.** Certainly okay for people with masochistic tendencies, but not for most people. Besides, it's a good way to get shot or mugged. You can't afford to lose good workers to a mugger.

6.   **Direct Mail and Email.** Wouldn't it be nice if we just sent out a letter and people joined? But what do we do with most of our junk mail?

    However, writing letters is a good way to pass the time and practice our spelling and handwriting. And if you are buying stamps, it helps support the Postal Service. But as a recruiting tool, let's leave it for the experienced mail-order and copy-writing professionals. And if someone joins because they think you have a cool email, then what is going to happen when that person gets a better-looking email?

7.   **Telephone Soliciting and Cold Calling.** It is 2 p.m. on Thursday afternoon. You have just managed to put your six-month-old baby to sleep. You are watching your favorite soap opera and they are about to announce the secret identity of the villain.

    The phone rings. What do you think your attitude would be when a stranger says he has randomly called you to be a distributor? People are so used to telephone solicitors trying to sell them something, that they just refuse to listen to any stranger's sales pitch. There surely must be an easier way.

8.   **Handouts and Flyers.** Almost every distributor in network marketing feels he has written the perfect

advertisement that will force the prospect to call and beg to be a distributor. He pastes them up, hands them out on corners, and slips them under doors.

While it may produce some activity of unqualified prospects, its real benefit is that the distributor gets a lot of fresh air and exercise. What do we normally do when people hand us flyers and junk mail? Is this the most efficient way of reaching qualified prospects? If the perfect network marketing advertisement existed, wouldn't everybody be recruited already?

And if advertising works, the company wouldn't need us.

9. **Grocery Store Bulletin Boards.** Just how many serious workers do you think read grocery store bulletin boards to find that **solid business opportunity?**

10. **Fund Raising.** Once the funds have been raised, you are left with zero distributors. Is this a way to build a solid organization? It is hard to convince an organization to use your product and hard to train them to sell it. Why put forth the effort for a one-time short-term benefit?

Big Al continued, "Surely there is some merit in each of these methods. If you have extra time, there is nothing wrong in doing them. But **do not deviate from The System.** Just because one person may have had success with one of these does not mean that you will encounter the same set of circumstances.

"Let me give you an example. At a convention, a young 17-year-old girl told of selling over $1,000 of products and sponsored several distributors by going door-to-door in her neighborhood in just one week. Everyone was excited that this young girl had shared with them the way to success.

"Needless to say, the other distributors failed. What the young girl failed to mention was that her mother was mayor of the small town, owned most of the property, and her tenants felt obligated to help her daughter.

"Another example: a young man confidently tells you about his success in helping a church raise funds through the sale of his products. What isn't mentioned is that his brother was the minister who ordered the members to sell this product.

"In other words, get all the facts. Most times there are special circumstances behind these inefficient methods of prospecting. Don't follow them blindly. **Use The System and let the amateur recruiters chase their tails trying to make these other methods work."**

The Traveling Salesman

The following week over coffee, Distributor Joe related an interesting situation. It seems that one of Joe's most promising distributors had a hot prospect 90 miles out of town. Since it took all evening driving there and back, there was no time for other appointments.

Even though the prospect wanted time to think it over, Joe was confident that he would join. Was it worth the time and effort to go out of town? Could the time be better spent making three or four presentations locally?

Big Al pulled out a blank piece of paper and began figuring. "Let's see now, 180 miles round trip at a cost of 50 cents a mile equals $90.00. You'll need a second trip to complete signing him up so that's another $90.00 for a total of $180.00. Joe, for that same $180.00, you could have bribed your next door neighbor to become a distributor and been home by 6:30 p.m.

"Plus, look at the income you lost by losing two evenings of sponsoring. How much money could you have made from those potential recruits you did not see because you were out of town? Add that figure to $180.00 and ask yourself if that out-of-town prospect was worth it.

"But that's not the whole story. How much time will you or your distributor lose by driving out of town to train this prospect? I personally sponsor people in my own backyard. You've heard the saying, **'The grass looks greener on the other side of the fence.'**

"Why not let amateur recruiters drive past 100,000 potential prospects on their way to see their out-of-town hot prospect? There will be plenty of these amateurs in your organization who do not wish to follow The System. Give them the leads and let them do the driving. As a professional recruiter, you have more important activities to occupy your time than driving."

Test Question: Distributor A, who lives in the city of Alpha, drives 100 miles to the city of Bimbo to recruit a new distributor. At the same time, Distributor B, who lives in Bimbo, drives 100 miles to the city of Alpha to recruit a new distributor.

Q. Who wins?

A. The gasoline station.

Big Al continued. "Think of it this way. Almost every person you meet is already pre-sold. People want more money in their lives and they want the benefits of our product. Our job is to simply not talk them out of it by giving terrible, untrained, boring presentations. You and I don't have to drive hundreds of miles to find a good prospect. Good prospects are everywhere."

One Story Is Worth 10,000 Facts

Big Al was sharpening Joe's presentation skills. "Don't just throw out facts, tell a story. Your prospects and distributors **will remember the story long after the facts have been forgotten.** And stories are more powerful and more motivating.

"Don't you want to motivate your prospect or distributor? I bet you can remember an interesting story told to you by your first grade teacher. But you have probably forgotten 90% of the facts you had to memorize in high school. Proof enough?

"And the best part is that stories engage people. When you are telling a story, people forget about you. They focus on the story. So if you want people to stop judging you, and to focus on the opportunity, tell a story."

Big Al then shared some examples of stories that were guaranteed to bring life to a conversation or presentation.

"Work Smart — Not Hard"
Story #1

If a president of a large conglomerate earns $1,000,000 a year and a common laborer earns $10,000 a year, does this mean the president worked 100 times harder? Did the president put in 100 times more hours in a week? I doubt if the president of any conglomerate could work a 400-hour week. Why is it then that some people earn much more than others?

They work smart — not hard.

These people have found ways to provide more service, to be more efficient ... ways to lead others to more productivity. In other words, they produce more value in the same allotted time.

Who would you pay more? A person who sells $100 worth of your goods or a person who sells $1,000 worth of your goods? Obviously, you would pay the second person 10 times more. If we wish to receive more income, we must produce more service. We must find ways of working smarter, not harder.

If I needed a one-mile-long ditch excavated, and was willing to pay $10,000, you could apply for the job. You would take your trusty shovel and begin digging. At the end of one year the ditch would be completed. For that one-mile ditch, I would then pay you $10,000 because you have performed $10,000 worth of service.

On the other hand, a friend of yours could apply for the job. Your friend then rents a ditch-digging machine for $100 and finishes the ditch in one day. Has he also provided $10,000 worth of service?

Who worked smart and who worked hard?

"Joe," said Big Al, "This story has several applications. You might tell this story to a prospect to impress on them that working for someone else is working hard, and having your own part-time business is working smart.

"You might use the story with a new distributor who spends all his time looking for new first-level distributors. That's working hard. Instead of trying to sponsor everyone personally, your new distributor should use The System, so he may only sponsor a few personally, but end up with hundreds in his organization. That's working smart."

"Proper Education"
Story #2

Let's look at how many years of our lives we spend in school:

Grade School	8 years
High School	4 years
College	4 years
Total:	16 years

College can cost about $30,000 per year. Why do we go to college? To become successful. But in college, we take English, Accounting, Business, Engineering, etc. These are all courses designed to make us good employees for someone else. We don't take a single course in our true major: **Success**.

We spend 16 years of our lives and $120,000 (four years in college) and don't take even one course in how to become a **Success**. Don't you think it would be worthwhile to spend $100 and two days to attend a course and learn how to become a **Success**?

Big Al explained, "The above story is useful in motivating a distributor to attend further skill and self-improvement training. It also can be tailored to new prospects.

"For example: 'Mr. Prospect, you've spent 16 years and $120,000 to learn how to be a good employee. Won't you invest $100 and two months to see if you can be as successful as your own boss?'"

"Here's Your Chance"
Story #3

Who makes more money? The person who owns the company or the employee who works for him? The owner, of course.

Mr. Prospect, you now have the opportunity to own your own business and decide how much money you can earn. Do you want to remain an employee and let your boss decide your earnings, or do you wish to start your own business by becoming a distributor now?

"The above story helps the prospect to make up his mind now. No need to think it over as the choice is clear; there is no middle ground," added Big Al.

"The Office Manager"
Story #4

A young mother decides to get a full-time job to pay the many bills that come with raising a family. There are many sacrifices she must make:

1. She will be away from the house for 8-10 hours a day. Housework and meals will suffer.

2. The children will no longer have the advantage of a full-time mother at home.

3. She will miss the wonderful experience of helping the children develop.

4. There will be less quality time with her family, as evenings are spent catching up on household duties.

But in return for these sacrifices, she finds a job paying $3,000 a month. After deductions, what does she really earn?

$3,000	**Salary**
-600	Federal income tax
-80	State income tax
-180	Social Security
-500	Monthly payment on second car
-60	Monthly insurance payment on second car
-80	Monthly maintenance on second car
-200	Gasoline to and from work
-600	Babysitter
-100	Beauty salon
-150	Increased wardrobe needs
-80	Insurance deductions and office gifts
-150	Meals
$220	**Remaining to pay bills**

That's earning less than $2 an hour. Is it worth 22 days a month away from the children and 176 hours of work, not counting travel time?

Wouldn't the young mother rather stay home if possible?

With our opportunity you can easily earn $220.00 from your home in just a few hours per week. Not only is it easier, more profitable, and fun, but you can now enjoy time with your family, too!

Big Al said, "The story about the young mother helps people appreciate time with their families."

"Oysters"
Story #5

Suppose that you are a professional pearl diver sitting on the dock by the sea. Every hour I give you a bucket of 100 oysters. Among the 100 oysters are five that have pearls. The other 95 are empty.

As a professional, you take out the first oyster, cut it open, and find it empty. You then carefully put it back together, hold it between your hands to keep it warm, and then sit there for days hoping it will grow a pearl. Is this what you'd do?

Of course not. You would throw the empty oyster away and reach for another and another until you found one with a pearl.

However, most distributors treat their friends and alleged "good prospects" like the empty oyster. Instead of going on to a good prospect, they keep hoping, asking, inviting, and pleading with the same people week after week. They will invite the same person 17 times to an opportunity meeting! They never catch a hint. They work too long with "empty oysters."

The secret to recruiting is not in convincing people, but in sorting people. You can wear yourself out and become discouraged, working with the same "empty oysters." Your job as a professional recruiter is only to sort through the prospects until you find one who wants to be a distributor. It is ten times easier to locate a prospect who wants to work, than to convince an unwilling disinterested prospect to work.

"The Eagle and the Oyster"
Story #6

Once there were two eggs discussing what they wanted to be when they hatch.

The first egg said, "I want to be an oyster when I hatch. An oyster just sits in the water. It has no decisions to make. The currents of the ocean move it about, so it doesn't have to plan. The ocean water that passes by is its food. Whatever the ocean provides is what the oyster may receive, no more, no less. That's the life for me. It may be limited, but there are no decisions, no responsibilities, just a plain existence controlled by the ocean."

The second egg said, "That's not the life for me. I wish to be an eagle. An eagle is free to go where he wants and do as he pleases. Sure he is responsible for hunting his own food and making survival decisions, but he is free to fly as high as the mountains. The eagle is in control, not controlled by others. I wish no limits placed on me. I do not wish to be a slave of the ocean. For this I am willing to pay the effort required to live the life of an eagle."

Which would you rather be an eagle or an oyster?

The above story is effective with prospects and distributors in a rut, who are complacent and just existing. It is designed to make them unhappy with the crumbs and limitations others throw their way, and to motivate them to make their own destinies.

"The Best Investment"
Story #7

Do you smoke? If you smoke cigarettes, a pack or more a day will cost you $70 a week. Do you drink coffee? Two cups a day will cost you about $40.00 a week. Yet how many distributors did those cigarettes and coffee get you?

None!

Why not invest $110 a week in your business? Learn new skills, go to the conventions, and get the tools you need to make your business soar.

The payoff is huge. You are spending the money already. Just redirect your money to get a better return on your investment.

"Two Young Men"
Story #8

There are two young men who are best friends. They grow up together. They go to school together. They become young men, and they both get good jobs in the same city.

One young man earns his regular salary. The other young man earns his regular salary, but once a month he gets a $1,000 bonus check from his part-time business.

"Which young man gets ahead financially?"

This story should at least open up the conversation. You might end up talking with your prospect about how one young man is a better saver. Or maybe you'll end up talking about how one young man gets an extra monthly check.

The story captures the imagination and interest of your prospect.

"Two Young Ladies"
Story #9

Two young ladies graduate from high school. One goes to university, graduates with $100,000 in debt and is unemployed. She hopes to get a job that will give her enough to live on, will never be able to pay off her debts, and if she raises a family, she will never see her family as she is commuting 5 or 6 days a week ... and then she retires a year before she dies.

The other young lady graduates from high school, starts her own network marketing business, and when her friend graduates from university, she retires.

"Facts tell. But stories sell."

Strawberry Fields Forever

Big Al continued teaching Distributor Joe about different stories.

"The real secret in communicating is using terms that your prospect will understand. How many times have you seen intelligent salesmen use high-tech terminology that sounds impressive to the prospect? While this sounds impressive, most times the prospect fails to buy because he does not understand the entire presentation.

"We must remember that if any part of our presentation fails to be clear, the natural tendency of the prospect is to delay a decision because of fear of the unknown.

"Here are some examples of network marketing terms that could confuse new prospects." (The prospect's interpretations in parentheses):

- Downline (an event to happen later on)

- PV (a rare disease as in, "Be careful not to catch a lot of PVs")

- BV (a more powerful strain of the disease)

- Upline, crossline, clothesline (it all sounds the same to them)

- Breakaway (leaving the network marketing business to do something else)

- Sponsor (free will donations to starving children overseas)

- Bonuses (the turkey given to company employees at Christmas)

- Distributor (the part that breaks and then your car won't start)

- Wholesaler (the meat packing plant on the other end of town)

- Overrides (4th gear on an automatic transmission)

"Any of the above words can be used in presentations. However, we must give proper explanations and be aware that our prospect may interpret something completely different. If you want to have a little fun, attend a group opportunity meeting and listen to the jargon used by the speaker. Notice the blank stare of the new prospects in the room. You'll probably be the only one laughing in the room, but at least you'll see a dramatic demonstration of bad communication.

"All this, of course, brings us to **strawberries**.

"The strawberry story is an excellent way to demonstrate how network marketing works to a beginner. Many times a beginner is reluctant to join because he questions the legitimacy or the legality of network marketing distribution. The strawberry story puts him at ease because it shows network marketing as an alternative way of distributing products to the familiar retail distribution system.

"So Joe, take the time to learn the story just in case you need it with a skeptical prospect."

The Strawberry Story

Let's say we want to buy strawberries from our local store. How did they get there?

First, the strawberries were picked at a small farm in the country and sold to the local co-op. Next, the co-op sold them to a large national distributor. The national distributor sells the strawberries to regional brokers who, in turn, resell them at a profit to local jobbers. The local jobbers sell the strawberries to large warehouses for the local grocery chains. The local chains then distribute them to the local grocery stores who mark up the price another 30-40% for overhead such as employee salaries, rent, advertising, insurance, utilities, inventory shrinkage, etc.

Each person along the way covers his overhead and adds on a profit. So while the strawberries may have cost only 25 cents in the field, the final price at the store is $1.00. This is known as the retail distribution method of marketing.

An alternative way of distribution is direct marketing or network marketing. Here the farmers (or manufacturers) sell the strawberries directly to the network marketing company. The network marketing company sells the strawberries directly to their distributors at wholesale. The distributors benefit by being able to purchase strawberries for their personal use at wholesale and can also make extra money by selling them to retail customers at retail.

This is a more direct way of marketing products, and by cutting out all the middle man profits, the network marketing company is able to pass these savings on to their distributors for additional profits called bonuses.

Bonuses work like this. If you bought strawberries at your local grocery store and liked them so much that you told your neighbor, your local store would receive additional sales because of your word-of-mouth advertising. The store, in its appreciation of your work, would then send you in the mail a word-of-mouth advertising bonus check the next day. Not very likely. The store has already spent its advertising budget in the local newspaper, so there is nothing left for you.

But in network marketing, it is all different!

If you liked the strawberries you purchased at wholesale from your network marketing company, then told your neighbor about them, and your neighbor became a distributor and purchased strawberries at wholesale from your network marketing company, you'd get a bonus! The network marketing company will give you a bonus for your effort that resulted in their increased sales.

That is why so many people are excited about network marketing. For doing what comes naturally (sharing a good deal or a good product) we get paid bonuses. Retail stores just can't compete when people find out about the tremendous advantages of network marketing. After all, if you liked the strawberries and told your neighbor, which would you choose:

Getting paid for it by a network marketing company or not getting paid by your local store?

The choice is clear: Network marketing or direct marketing is a better deal for us.

The Two Magic Questions

Distributor Joe said, "Those stories are just great, but sometimes I have trouble getting started. I need something to break the ice. I've tried talking about the weather and sports, but that's a waste of time and the prospect knows it.

"Besides, I'm uncomfortable saying, 'The weather sure is nice, how about looking at this business opportunity?' That doesn't flow at all.

"Plus, if there was a way to break the ice and qualify the prospect at the same time, I could save lots of time by only talking to interested, qualified people. I seem to be making a lot of presentations to people who are totally uninterested. Do you have a solution?"

Big Al had the answers. He was a pro. He used The System.

Big Al replied, "You can **save a lot of time by pre-qualifying your prospects.** At the same time you can also 'break the ice' and get down to business. But first let's take a look at the qualities a prospect must have to be a distributor.

"Intelligence? No, you and I have both sponsored some smart people and some ... well, not-so-smart people. A good salesman? No, we know some successful distributors who are both shy and unassuming. A positive attitude? Not a chance. There are plenty of negative distributors in the world.

"There are really two very important qualities the prospect should have to become a good distributor."

#1. Desire.

"The prospect must have the desire to earn some extra money. However, the biggest mistake amateur recruiters make is confusing **need** with **desire**. They are completely different. Many times, people who need extra money have no desire to earn it.

"The amateur recruiter concentrates on all the unemployed and 'broke' people who do not wish to put forth an extra effort to get ahead. This could also include people with dead-end jobs who only want to watch TV in the evening.

"An unemployed person may need extra money, but may not have the desire to go out and earn it. He may be satisfied just where he is. The amateurs spend endless hours trying to reprogram needy people who do not have desire. Playing psychologist may be good for the ego but bad for the wallet."

#2. Time.

"Everyone has 24 hours in a day. What we are looking for is someone who is **willing** to set aside time to work your business opportunity. You may find people with nothing to do who insist they just can't set aside the time. TV, Internet browsing, etc., are just too important to give up. These prospects are not for us.

"We want prospects who can commit to six or ten hours a week for their business. If someone really busy says he can only set aside four hours a week, that's okay too. At least he made a commitment. Besides, busy people get things done."

Big Al continued, "Now that we know the qualities required of a good distributor, it's easy to find out if they qualify. All we have to do is ask. For example:

Q. Do you want to earn some extra money?

Q. Are you willing to set aside six to ten hours per week?

"We just **listen** to their answers to determine if they qualify. Just that simple. With these two magic questions we also 'break the ice' and are immediately down to business.

"The magic really isn't in the questions. The magic is in the answers. Pay close attention to what your prospect says and **how** he says it."

Distributor Joe made a note to use the two magic questions on his very next appointment. With this new information, Joe felt he was getting close to becoming a recruiting pro.

The Big Payoff

Big Al spent one entire evening showing Distributor Joe the "Big Picture."

"The really big distributor organizations are not made up of one superstar who personally recruited 1,000 distributors. Instead, they consist of one professional recruiter who sponsored a few good distributors and helped each of them get 100-200 distributors into their organizations.

"Wouldn't a person feel better having five to ten self-sufficient, well-trained "Generals" with properly-trained organizations, than to have 1,000 untrained, unmotivated "Privates" with no organizations?

"Here is how we get those deep, secure, profitable organizations."

1. We work as a team with our personally-enrolled distributor (who is a worker, not an unmotivated distributor) until we have built at least 15 distributors in his group.

2. We help our first-level distributor identify two, three or more good workers he can work with as a team.

3. Because our first-level distributor may not be able to work with each of his own workers immediately, we help by teaming with some of his workers. Even though we are now teaming with our second- or third-level distributors, we are still building our organization by training and recruiting more downline distributors.

4.   The System will give us the following distributors per worker:

(a) 1 worker (our personally-enrolled distributor)

(b) 2 or 3 new workers in training

(c) 12 or 13 unmotivated distributors/product users.

"If we can just train and develop six or seven good workers, we will develop hundreds of distributors in our organization as they duplicate our success."

1.   We make sure each worker in our organization understands how The System works. Don't invest time pushing and offending an unmotivated distributor who is happy just using the products. We then review The System with our workers on a regular basis to help them stay on track.

2.   Only after our present protégé's organization is fully trained do we add another protégé. We don't spread ourselves too thin, and we must finish what we've started.

Big Al asked if there were any questions.

Joe replied, "None at all, Big Al. My group is over 300 already and I'm not deviating one step from The System. I always make presentations with someone else. And with the information I've received, I'm beginning to become a recruiting pro just like you."

Close Before You Start

Big Al and Distributor Joe were reviewing the previous week's work.

Distributor Joe asked, "Big Al, earlier in my training you told me how prospects make their decision **before** I start my presentation. Is there some way to manage and control these important seconds before the presentation begins?"

"You are right," Big Al replied. "Most of our effectiveness comes with what we say before we start our presentation.

"If we don't prepare our prospect properly, our prospect will be looking for reasons **not** to join. Prospects want to prepare excuses to use against high-pressured salespeople.

"If your prospect is on the defensive and looking for reasons **not** to join, your prospect isn't listening to all the good things our business has to offer. This is why salesmen have such a hard time communicating with their prospects.

"Let me give you an example of just one solution to this universal sales problem.

"Merely put the prospect at ease by telling him:

1.   Most people buy your product.

2.   The total cost of your product.

3.   "Reasons" why he shouldn't buy.

4. That you will just present the facts and then it's up to him.

"The secret is to tell the prospect these four things **BEFORE** you make your sales presentation."

Here are two examples of the above technique:

1. Mr. Prospect, most people I talk with join Acme Network Marketing because they see how this can really help their incomes. After all, the total cost of getting started in our program is only $49.00. That's less than the cost of a good newspaper ad. As a matter of fact, the only two reasons people don't join are: they don't really understand our program; or that times are so tough, they just can't afford $49.00 right away. What I'm going to do is just present to you the basic facts about our opportunity and if you like it, fine, we'll get started. If you don't like it, fine, that's okay too. Fair enough?

2. Mr. Prospect, most people just love our fabulous Acme Widget Product. They're always telling their friends about it. After all, it only costs $30.00 and that works out to only $1.00 a day, less than a cheap cup of coffee if you think about it. You know, the only reasons people don't buy the fabulous Acme Widget Product is that they just can't believe how well it works, or they just can't afford the $30.00. Anyway, let me show you how it works and if you like it, fine, buy one and surprise your wife. If you don't like it, that's okay too. Fair enough?

"By using this simple four-step technique **BEFORE** your sales presentation, your closing ratio will increase dramatically. Here is why this technique works wonders with your prospect."

1. You have told your prospect that most people buy your product or opportunity. Your prospect does not want to be the first one to try it. He wants to know if others have made the decision to buy. Since most people buy your product, the prospect's natural tendency is to want to join the majority.

2. You have told your prospect the total cost of your product unlike most salesmen he has encountered. They usually hide the price and spring it out at the very end of their presentation. The prospect worries throughout the entire presentation when the price will be revealed to him and how much it will be. By revealing the price first, his mind is now clear to listen to your product's features and benefits.

3. You build trust and confidence in your prospect by telling him the entire cost in the beginning. He looks upon you as an honest businessman, not as a salesman that holds back information and tries to trick him. Even if your price is "high" or "shocking," he will want to hear about your product to see why it is so good to command such a price.

4. This technique gives you a more unbiased, low-pressure, "I don't care" approach versus the high-pressure, "You have to buy it" approach. The prospect's defenses will go down when he sees that you are not attacking his jugular vein. When handled properly, this low-key approach motivates your prospect to want to qualify for your product. He starts selling himself.

5. By giving your prospect "reasons" not to buy, you have taken the pressure off. He doesn't have to fight you about why he should not buy, because he knows you'll accept those reasons. By removing this fear, your prospect can now listen and concentrate on the features and benefits of your presentation.

6. If you plan properly, the "reasons" not to buy really force the prospect to buy. In the above two examples we have subtly said to the prospect, "Everyone buys unless he doesn't understand or is too poor." This also helps you isolate objections at the end of your presentation. Your prospect either needs more information or he just doesn't have the money.

7. By telling your prospect that it's okay if he buys or not, you again are relieving the sales pressure he naturally places on himself. However, by his agreeing to "Fair enough?" he is committing himself to a decision NOW. This helps prevent the "I'll think it over" objection when used properly.

Closing Is Easy When You Do This

Big Al continued to help Distributor Joe each week with his closing skills. Big Al showed how little it took to get a decision.

"When you say there are **two types of people in the world**, your prospect will immediately forget all his drama and skepticism, and anxiously wait to see what the two types of people in the world are, and which type he is.

"People are curious. They don't want to go on with their lives unless they know about these two types of people. Use this curiosity to hold their attention.

"But it gets better. When you say **there are two types of people in the world**, your prospect will make a mental decision about which group he belongs to. This helps in closing."

Big Al went on to give Distributor Joe some examples.

1. There are two types of people in the world, those that are open-minded and looking for opportunity, and those that have given up on life. (This is a great way to handle tough prospects that are resistant.)

2. There are two types of people in the world, those that resign themselves to a lifetime of commuting to work, and those that would love to work from their homes.

3. There are two types of people in the world, those that would love to be their own boss and set their own hours, and those that are okay with just a few weeks of vacation every year.

4. There are two types of university graduates in the world, those that want to start a part-time business so they can eventually be their own boss, and those that resign themselves to 45 years of hard labor working for someone else.

5. There are two types of office workers in the world, those that work hard so their boss has a big house for his retirement, and those that want to retire early and have the retirement of their dreams.

6. There are two types of people in the world, those that are okay with working five and six days a week on a job, and those that want five-day weekends every week.

7. There are two types of people in the world, those that get to travel, experience and see the world, and those that only get to see the world on the travel channels on their televisions.

Big Al continued, "Just a few short words such as 'There are two types of people in the world' can help your prospect to instantly make a decision to take advantage of the business you offer.

"And, you can use the same words for products and services. Here are some examples."

1. There are two types of people in the world, those that use our magic night cream and make their skin younger while they sleep, and those that wrinkle a little bit more every night.

2. There are two types of people in the world, those that wake up every morning feeling like a million dollars, and those that crawl out of bed with aches and pains, feeling a lot older than they are.

3. There are two types of grandmothers in the world, those that dread the visit of their little home-wrecking

grandchildren, and those grandmothers that have so much energy that their grandchildren whine, "Grandma, slow down. We can't keep up!"

4. There are two types of people in the world, those that love to travel and experience the world, and those that have to stay home and just read about it.

5. There are two types of people in the world, those that have to drive to get overpriced gourmet coffee, and those that save money by being able to have gourmet coffee with them any time they want.

6. There are two types of dieters in the world, those that starve themselves, eat funny food, exercise, and watch their weight come back ... and those that lose weight easily by just changing what they have for breakfast.

Big Al continued, "Joe, you will learn more powerful closing techniques as you grow, but for now, remember this. Just a few simple words before you start will make closing your prospect easy."

How To Make Unsuccessful Recruiting Presentations

Distributor Joe asked Big Al, "Two-on-one presentations are so easy. But what is the best way to do a full presentation? For example, maybe I have to do an opportunity meeting for a group of people. I know the meeting should at least be 20 or 30 minutes. What should I say? What should I talk about most?"

"It's not enough to just memorize a successful recruiting presentation," said Big Al. "You must understand the principles and the psychology behind great presentations.

"In order to do that, let's look at a presentation given by someone else. Obviously, we can't all sit in on a two-on-one presentation, so let's attend a business opportunity meeting given by a leader with another company. We want to watch someone who is confident, can speak in front of a group, has attained some degree of success, and would generally be considered in the top 5%."

That Monday night Big Al and Distributor Joe attended an opportunity meeting for "Wonderful Products." They both sat in the back row so they could take careful notes of both the speaker and the crowd reaction.

They chose this meeting because it had a reputation of being exciting and the very best in town. With notepads in hand, they patiently waited as the meeting started 35 minutes late to allow for latecomers. Big Al mentioned that starting late is really punishing the distributors who come on time while rewarding those who are tardy. Finally, the meeting started.

The opening speaker introduced himself and immediately began to tell the audience how great he was. He mentioned that he was in the top 5% of all people because he thought like a winner. Obviously, the people in the audience were losers because they were not presently distributors for this wonderful company and the speaker told the audience they needed to have their thinking changed.

After 20 minutes of explaining why the listeners were only sheep being led to a financial slaughter, the speaker finally got around to naming the company and began telling about its wonderful founders.

One founder grew up in a log cabin and suffered defeat after defeat. Only through superhuman effort was he able to overcome these hardships and develop his own philosophy on life. This philosophy was to become the backbone of the company, and the only purpose for the company was to share this wonderful knowledge with others. The company was not in business to make a profit, but to change the minds of humanity.

The other founder's ancestry was revealed in explicit detail for 10 minutes, and then his long list of academic achievements was read. His long journeys to ancient tombs and cultures, his knowledge of ancient manuscripts, and his elaborate testing techniques were cited. One lady in the crowd stood up and cheered with tears in her eyes, explaining how the products had changed her life. At least this woke up the audience.

After another 15 minutes of homage to the founders, the speaker invited the distributors present to come to the front of the room to explain the products and share their experiences.

The first distributor said he really hadn't been a distributor long enough to try the products, but knew of someone who had taken them and recovered from cancer, senility and hardening of the arteries within one week by swallowing 42 tablets a day.

The next distributor told how you could make millions in just a few short weeks with this wonderful pyramid concept. In fact, you didn't even have to use or like the products. All you had to do was get others to invest in a kit and everyone would get rich. A few members of the audience clapped loudly and yelled, "Go for it!"

The next distributor said he didn't like the taste of the product, but felt it helped enough people so it wouldn't be a problem for anyone in the business. About that time a few guests in the audience looked at their watches, and quietly crept out the back door.

The next distributor told of his personal experience. He had been blind, deaf, crippled and next to death until he drank the Wonderful Super Juice. In two weeks' time he was completely healed and had qualified for the Olympic marathon. Two "business types" in the audience rolled their eyes and looked at their potential sponsor, thinking, "What is this?" The distributor then proceeded to ask the audience to sing the "Wonderful Products" healing song.

Finally, the next speaker stood and announced that he was going to talk about the marketing plan. After 90 minutes of questionable information, the audience was relieved to see the meeting finally get to the point. However, several people did leave because of other commitments or baby-sitting problems. The marketing plan of Wonderful Products was revealed to the remaining group:

First, a person becomes a qualified advisor counselor at captain level. After accumulating "wonderful points" the person could receive 4% of the 6% training bonus on unqualified private non-advisor distributors on every even-number calendar month.

When a person reached a total BV of 60% of his personal group's PV, not counting bonus product points, he then could move to a 70% level of net profit on single case sales. The "blue moon" convention points were completely different, though. In that case, a person would come into the program as a non-qualified distributor and qualify through a unique "general direct supervisory plan." Finally, this decision should be made immediately as the charter month would end tomorrow.

After 30 minutes of detailed explanation of the finer points of the the Wonderful Products marketing plan, the speaker invited another person to the front of the room to tell his personal story.

Ten minutes later, this speaker was so confused that he began to panic and said, "Are there any questions?"

Once he opened the meeting to questions, question after question came from the audience until 11:15 p.m. when the speaker finally said, "Okay, we better call this meeting to an end as many people have to go to work tomorrow."

The remaining five people in the audience nodded in agreement, rushed to their cars and sped home.

The Answer To Inefficient Recruiting Presentations

Big Al and Distributor Joe went to a local coffee shop to discuss the three-hour opportunity meeting they had just attended.

"Absolutely amazing!" commented Distributor Joe. "I have never seen a more disorganized and unprofessional excuse for a business presentation. I didn't know whether to be sick or to laugh. The most intelligent people at the meeting were the guests. At least they had the common sense to leave halfway through the presentation. I can see why there is really no competition in network marketing. Anyone who takes just a little time to learn the basics can leave the majority miles behind."

Big Al nodded in agreement and said, "Joe, you have watched me give many a presentation and have given plenty on your own with your own group. You have been copying my basic presentation, but now is a good time to learn why we have structured our presentation the way we have.

"As you know, the final decision by the prospect usually occurs way before the presentation. But that is still no excuse for a miserable presentation to our prospects.

"A full presentation with all of the facts, such as the one you would do at a hotel opportunity meeting, should only last 25-30 minutes. We should go right to the core of the information the new prospect wants to know. You may have noticed that our presentations have five key sections. Each key section is designed to answer one of the five key questions that every new prospect has in order to make the decision to join. Let's review these sections so that you will better understand the science of professional network marketing business presentations.

"And for this example, we are going to assume that our prospect has never heard of network marketing, so we will have to explain even the basics."

SECTION 1: THE INDUSTRY

Our prospects will want to know what kind of industry we are in. They may have a particular aversion to certain industries such as insurance or real estate. We can answer this first question in their minds very easily. We simply tell them we are in network marketing. There are two types of prospects, those who understand what network marketing is and those who don't.

For those familiar with network marketing, we have just answered their question and we can go quickly on to Section Two. For those who don't understand what network marketing is, we simply tell them the Strawberry story. This story legitimizes the direct marketing concept and makes them feel comfortable with this alternative way of getting products and services to the public. We certainly want our prospects to be relaxed, don't we?

Section 1 of our presentation should only take three or four minutes at the most.

SECTION 2: THE COMPANY

Our prospect is not interested in a complete financial audit, the number of square feet in the executive washroom, the founder's mother's ancestry, the credentials of the quality control foreman, or the quality of paper used in the shipping and receiving room. His real desire is to know just the name of the company, if its management has some experience, and if the company is growing and has good plans for the future. In other words, are they good guys or bad guys?

Too many presentations get carried away with a lot of credibility statistics that should be saved for training. At this point in our new prospect's career, he just wants to know a few facts, not the company's entire history. His questions about the company can usually be answered in about one minute.

SECTION 3: THE PRODUCTS

Frequently the excited new distributor tells the new prospect what excites the new distributor, and that's not what the prospect wants and needs to hear. When a new distributor gets started, he is usually totally sold on his products. In his excitement he feels that the new prospect must listen to every testimonial, every test data report, and every feature of every individual product his company carries. This process can take many hours and usually puts the prospect to sleep if he can't find the energy to get away.

What the prospect really wants to know is, "Is there a market for the products? Will they sell?" Our entire product presentation should center not on the price, quality and test reports of the product, but on how people are using them and enjoying them right now. We must answer the prospect's question. Sure, the other factors are important, but let's be professional and answer the question that will help the prospect decide if this business opportunity is for him.

Our product presentation should take about five to eight minutes. We are just giving an overview of individual products or product lines, not a complete product training workshop.

SECTION 4: TRAINING

This is the difference between professional recruiting presentations and those pathetic amateur attempts to present the business opportunity. Have you ever wondered why the following scenario happens?

A new distributor's prospect sits through an entire meeting for an hour. At the end of the meeting, he turns to his prospective sponsor and says, "Boy, those products are really great, and that marketing plan sure looks like the way to financial security. The amount of money to be made in this business is phenomenal! By the way, I am not going to join."

Why does this happen? Simple.

The person giving the presentation forgot to answer the most important question of the entire meeting: "CAN I DO IT?"

Our new prospect would certainly want all the benefits offered by our program, but he has never been in network marketing before, or has been previously unsuccessful at it. Therefore, we must answer his question, "Can I do it?" if we are to sponsor him into our program. We do this by explaining our training program.

Our training program consists of the literature, books, CDs, etc. available from the company. Also available are the many local training meetings in his area. We strongly encourage him to attend to **begin** his learning process, but this is only the first part of our training.

Part Two is the "On The Job" training. We ask him to only set a few appointments and watch or observe while we sponsor new distributors into his organization. We are building his group while he is watching! What could be easier for him?

Our new prospect will now feel more at ease knowing that he can attend training sessions and observe his sponsor building his organization. Our new prospect will now realize that this is a business that he can do. With this assurance our prospect is ready to go with our program even before he hears about the money.

More distributors make an excited decision to join during these vital five minutes of training explanation than all other parts of the presentation combined.

SECTION 5: MARKETING PLAN

The last five or ten minutes of our presentation should be dedicated to explaining how our compensation program works. Our prospect will have three questions concerning this area:

How much will it cost me?

What do I have to do?

How much money can I make?

By answering, "How much will it cost me?" right away, it will put our prospect at ease. Most salesmen will wait to the very end to spring the price on a prospect. We will do just the opposite. We don't want our prospect thinking throughout our presentation, "How much is this going to cost me?"

"What do I have to do?" has already been answered in the training section. Just set a few appointments and watch us build your group!

"How much can I make?" is easy. We just give a quick overview of our marketing plan and maybe provide a few examples of what others have done in the business.

Big Al continued, "That's all there is to a great, professional presentation. No mystery at all. If we just answer our prospect's five basic questions, we will sponsor with ease. And the best part is that is usually takes less than 25 or 30 minutes!

"And don't worry about the close. When we are done, all we have to do is just ask him if this is for him or not. There is really very little reason to think it over. All the questions have been answered. No need for high pressure.

"So Joe, for now, this is a good template for you to follow. Later when we have time, I will help you improve on this basic template. As your skills get better, you will learn how to do a "One-Minute Presentation" and a "Two-Minute Story Presentation" that will go directly to the decision-making part of your prospect's brain. But for now, you are already in the top 1% in skills, so let's perfect what we have already learned."

Distributor Joe again took careful notes and planned to attend another competitor's network marketing meeting the following week. It was cheap entertainment and Distributor Joe always enjoyed a good laugh.

I Need More Volume!

"I love this business," said Distributor Joe. "But I need more volume in my group so I can get a bigger bonus check! What should I do?"

Big Al smiled. "Every network marketing distributor has posed this same question sometime in his network marketing career. Let me show you the wrong way, and then the right way to get more volume."

Distributor Joe grabbed his notepad. The lesson was about to begin.

Option #1: Train the present distributor force to increase volume.

This is the most popular option tried by network marketing distributors. Distributors think they can teach each distributor in their group to buy and sell even more products. The group leader thinks:

1. If each distributor loved the products as much as I do, it would be easy to raise the volume. All I have to do is teach them the 44 different ways they could use more products.

2. If each distributor knew as much about selling as I do, then of course they could sell more products to their friends.

3. If my training could motivate all those non-motivated distributors that I have accumulated over

my career, just think of the tremendous potential increase in my group's volume. The only thing holding me back could be the inspiration of my distributors.

So we decide to implement this three-step process with our group. Here is what happens.

We introduce a product training program for three Thursday nights in a row. At least that much time is needed to learn the ingredients, test reports, testimonials, and company literature. We have homework, weekly tests, and demonstrations. Those attending are our core group of distributors who always show up for every meeting, most times without a new guest or recruit, but they appreciate the new insight into the product line. As a matter of fact they are so impressed with our training that they insist we immediately move on to the retail sales training we promised.

Our retail training is scheduled for Saturdays from 9 a.m. to 2 p.m. for four Saturdays in a row. We want to build solid closing skills, learn to handle objections, AIDA formulas, facts, features, benefits, etc. We incorporate role-playing, sales contests, memorize product line presentations, etc. Our newly trained group is so good that you can't say "Hello" without them putting a trial close on you.

Now our group is ready for a full-fledged recruiting workshop. Wouldn't it be nice to use all these new sales skills on some potential new distributors? On Monday nights we schedule a 7 p.m. to 10 p.m. recruiting class for the next five weeks. We will cover prospecting, closing, openers, interest steps, advertising, direct mail, closing and starting our new distributors. After all, what better sponsor could a new distributor have than a well-trained, mature pro in our business?

After our recruiting training, we notice our graduates are not producing new distributors on a regular basis. Seems they have been spending all their time at training workshops. It appears that they are setting a poor personal example and could use some leadership training. We employ a consultant who charges our distributors $375 per person to put them through an intense, two-weekend seminar to teach them the principles that make great leaders. The team-building rope exercises in the woods are particularly entertaining. After all, how can they build a large organization if they are unable to lead?

Then it finally hits us.

We have developed a mature force of old-time distributors, who know everything about the product, can give credible presentations to a new prospect, have excellent sales skills, and know how to be a good leader, but are not motivated to do a thing.

With this fact staring us in the face, we truly see that all of our previous training has been for naught, wasted totally. All the skills in the world mean nothing if our distributors are not motivated to go out, overcome their fears, and do something. What we have is a group of professional students, always going to classes and training so they won't have to go out in the real world to do the work.

And why should they? In all the training classes, they never get rejection and are surrounded by positive people. It's much more fun.

We have a tired old mature distributor force of professional meeting-goers who enjoy the fellowship and social life our business offers. They are so afraid of rejection on their way to success that they are constantly going to seminars, workshops, classes, etc., to keep themselves busy, so they will not have to face the real world with its objections and rejections.

What is our solution? Let's forget and throw away all our training and instead have one really good training on motivation.

If we can get our people motivated, results would follow. We have seen many new distributors with no sales, recruiting, or product skills go out and build large businesses because they were motivated to do it. Our group of loyal groupies lacks the motivation to overcome their fears.

Therefore they do nothing. They enjoy going to so many meetings there is no time left to go out and use the information and skills learned.

We are basically training them to death.

If motivation is our solution, we will go out and get the best motivational speaker we can find and book him or her for an all-day Saturday seminar to really psyche our troops up, to get them to realize their potential, to believe in themselves, to go out and do it!

The big day arrives and the only people there are our core group of over-trained groupies. However, this time things are different. Our group is standing on chairs, screaming success slogans, making new commitments, setting goals, getting the spirit and really getting motivated. They are slapping each other on the back saying how great they feel, how great everyone there is, and believing with conviction they now are truly going to the top. Our formerly tired, mature groupies are now goal-oriented, motivated doers, and just can't wait to leave and go out and do it.

On Saturday evening they go home and re-define their goals. They spread the word with their family that finally they can expect big things from the business.

Sunday being a day of rest, our newly motivated distributors make good use of the time mapping their plan of action and listening again to a good motivational audio.

Monday is a workday, but our motivated distributor gets home and the first challenge is who to approach first. After reviewing the prospect list, he determines Fred and Joe would be good first targets. Fred reminds him that he has been invited at least 15 times to an opportunity meeting and is serious about his non-interest.

Undaunted, our distributor jumps up and down and yells, "I feel great!" and for good measure, jumps off a chair or two. Why let Fred ruin our motivation?

The next phone call goes to Joe, who says he can't meet tonight because the big Monday Night Football game is coming on in 30 minutes. Our motivated distributor takes the hint, and decides to watch the game also, since he had completely forgotten about this important game in his goal-setting excitement.

Tuesday night brings the same results. One or two phone calls to some old prospects confirms his suspicions that no one is really interested in the business.

Wednesday is church night and on Thursday, everyone is planning for the weekend.

Weekends are definitely not the time to recruit as people are spending time with their families and enjoying the two days off their jobs.

Option #1: Train the present distributor force to increase volume isn't working.

So what is the real solution to the problem of how to get more volume?

To Get More Milk,
You Have To Get More Cows!

You can't get more milk from cows by squeezing harder.

The real solution to getting more milk is to get more cows.

Squeezing a few extra dollars from your present distributors will never get that big increase in volume you are looking for.

You can get ten times the results by using your efforts to locate new distributors rather than squeezing a few drops more out of your present group.

So why don't leaders spend this valuable time looking for new distributors?

Fear of rejection.

It is easy to spend time teaching your present group and getting compliments that you are so smart and wonderful. Unfortunately, this doesn't grow your business fast. Many times it only gives you a warm feeling and provides entertainment for your distributors. If you are in business for a good warm feeling, this would be nice; but if you are looking for a business profit and to increase volume, this continuous training is a cruel joke on both you and your distributors.

Sponsoring new recruits is not as safe or easy. Sometimes you are unsure or risk rejection when prospects say, "No." Many times you feel that if you just could go back to the sheltered environment of your present, pre-sold group, you would feel happier.

It is easy to agree that sponsoring new distributors is better, but hard to implement. Of course, we should all stop visiting and socializing with our present group of distributors. Sure, we should go out and get new distributors. More cows mean more milk.

However, there are several things that might make us uneasy. No leads, fears, no credibility with strangers, little sales experience, and no plan for success.

The solution is using the "Two-on-One" sales presentation. The distributor contacts a friend or acquaintance, and we simply make the presentation. We do not suffer the loss of confidence by receiving rejection, so we are in a good state of mind to make the presentation. All our distributor has to do is make the appointment, and sit back and watch. This is the power of The System as it overcomes the fears and problems of cold recruiting, also known as "One-on-One."

Another important factor in getting new recruits is that new recruits have enthusiasm. It is very difficult to get old pros excited and enthusiastic. They have been around and have seen it all. They have already approached all their friends with their initial excitement and will normally just sit in a holding pattern of mediocrity.

How many times have we seen an unskilled, brand-new distributor outperform the old pro just on his enthusiasm and excitement? Want to put new life into your group? Get new distributors. They will increase the entire group's activity and excitement.

Groups grow faster by spurts or by campaigns. You have to get the momentum going, but once started, the group will grow geometrically. We have all seen a group explode in size when everyone is excited and confident. And the confidence keeps growing as people bring in more and more new people, fueling the fire of the group.

The secret is to start this fire or sponsoring campaign by re-committing yourself to numerous Two-on-One presentations. Your goal is to set an example to light this recruiting explosion.

To summarize, don't waste your time over-training and over-socializing with your distributors. The only true route to building bigger volume is to get more distributors, not by squeezing your present distributors harder.

To get more milk, get more cows!

Something for Nothing

Big Al taught Distributor Joe many lessons. For Joe, this particular lesson helped him deal with unmotivated prospects.

"The Something for Nothing Lesson."

What if we walked into our local bank one day and made the following proposition to the bank officer:

"I would like to deposit $100,000 into a Certificate of Deposit. I want to begin drawing interest on it immediately. However, I am not ready to make the deposit now, but you can start making the interest payments to me immediately."

The banker would probably say, "No way! You must make the deposit before you can start earning the interest."

As silly as this example sounds, we contact many prospects every month who wish for the same thing.

They want the rewards first, before they deposit the effort.

Have you ever heard the following statements by distributors and prospects?

- "I don't want to buy any product this month. Let me wait until next month to see if I will have a big enough bonus check."

- "If I had a bigger bonus check, then I would get excited."

- "This sounds like a lot of hard work. It may take several months before I could reap the rewards."

- "The meeting is too far away. Why don't you go and just tell me what happened?"

- "If you promise to build a big group for me, then I'll consider joining."

- "Let the company come out with a new advertising campaign that will get distributors flocking to my door. That is when I'll start working."

- "If my group was doing better, then I could afford to help them grow."

- "Why should I invest in products and sales aids? I haven't made any money yet."

The list can go on and on. People always seem to want something for nothing.

Wouldn't it be nice if companies paid us before we worked? Sure it would. But let's be realistic. If we are going to make it as **leaders**, we must help our prospects and distributors understand that **reward follows effort**. There is no free lunch.

Distributor Joe Makes a Difference

As Distributor Joe continued building his business using the System, he earned more than money. He earned the satisfaction of knowing that he helped change other people's lives.

Joe learned that there was more to network marketing than just the bonus check. For some, it was a sense of community. For others it was a passion for sharing products with others. And for many, they just loved being around positive people instead of their negative in-laws. They loved the self-improvement atmosphere.

So now when Joe shared his opportunity with others, he could tell stories about people he helped that they could identify with. Here are a few of Joe's stories.

Boring Bob.

Bob wasn't dynamic; in fact, he was often accused of being personality-free. As a conservative accountant, Bob was interested in what just a few hundred dollars a month could do to enhance his retirement.

Before network marketing, Bob's total retirement would be $2,200 each month. Not bad, but not enough for all of his expenses.

So here is what Bob did. He built a small group that earned him $500 each month. With his $500 extra a month, he paid off his house mortgage early. Now, he no longer had that $900 per month mortgage payment.

With just that one change of removing his $900 mortgage payment, and with the addition of $500 extra a month, Bob could now retire comfortably.

Bob said, "Now I can go fishing and visit my grandchildren instead of having a part-time job just to pay my expenses."

Married Mary.

Mary had a problem. Day care expenses, second car payments, a job that meant she had no time for her family.

Distributor Joe helped Mary create a $1,500 per month income. That was enough to quit her job since she would no longer need a second car and no longer need day care for her children.

Mary's comment to Joe? "I hated paying other people to watch my children grow up. I wanted to be their full-time mother."

Traveling Tim.

Tim had a passion to travel and experience the world. Only two problems.

1. Tim had a job. That took up most of his week.

2. Tim didn't have any extra money to travel so he simply sat at home and dreamed about traveling.

Distributor Joe introduced Tim to the exciting possibilities of network marketing. It took two years, but

Tim was eventually able to quit his job and travel seven days a week. Tim's comment?

"Every day for me is a holiday."

Heather pays off her student loans.

Heather was only a freshman in college, but she could see that her education loans would be over $100,000 at the end of just four years. That would be a huge debt hanging over her when she graduated.

Instead of getting a traditional, low-paying part-time job, Heather began doing network marketing. While her first year was difficult, she was just learning, and her second year was better. The extra check she earned was enough that she didn't have to borrow much money for her second year of education.

In year three, her networking business paid all of her college expenses, plus started to pay back her previous college loans.

In year four, not only did she pay back all of her college loans, she had extra money for a comfortable senior year at college.

When Heather graduated from college, her network marketing checks were enough for her to live comfortably, so she retired.

Heather commented to Joe, "My friends graduated in debt, unemployed, hoping to get a job that will take up almost every day of their lives. Their reward for graduating from college is 45 years of hard labor. Thank you for helping me have a different life."

Oscar changes his life.

Oscar was 55 years old and only now began to seriously think about his retirement. Throughout his working career he never saved or planned for his upcoming retirement, and now was suddenly struck with the problem of very little time, and a lot to accomplish. Distributor Joe had to help him produce a retirement income in just seven years.

Fortunately Oscar had something to start with. His company pension plan offered $500 a month. While this was just a pittance, it was better than nothing.

Oscar thought about all those years that he believed that the company would take care of him in his retirement. What a joke! Seven years from now when he is ready to retire, $500 probably will barely pay the utility bills.

Oscar would also be eligible for Social Security benefits when he retired. His benefits were calculated to be $1,500 per month. "At least I'll be getting something back for all those years I paid in," Oscar thought.

Now a $2,000 a month retirement is not a lot of money, but it is more than many people have when they retire. After food, auto expenses, rent or mortgage payments, etc., $2,000 would barely provide minimum needs. "How can I save and make up for lost time?" Oscar thought.

Distributor Joe helped Oscar get started in network marketing, and while not very successful, Oscar did manage to net about $800 every month.

Oscar systematically saved this for one year and used his $9,600 savings as a small downpayment on a house next door. The house was rented for $1,200 a month and after taxes, insurance, and minor expenses, there was a little money left to service the mortgage.

Oscar then took his $800 part-time income to pay off the mortgage earlier. In a few years, Oscar had completely paid off the house next door.

Now he had a plan.

He next purchased another house down the street. Oscar used his $800 part-time network marketing income, plus the rent from his other property to pay off this house mortgage in record time. Now Oscar owned two houses with no debt.

So how did Oscar's retirement look like when he turned age 65?

Company pension plan: $500
Social Security: $1500
Rent from two houses: $2200
Network marketing income: $800

TOTAL INCOME: $5,000

On a retirement income of $5,000 a month, Oscar lived comfortably ever after.

Network Marketing Leader's Note: Just think of the retirement income Oscar could have accumulated if he had started just eight or ten years earlier. By reinvesting the income of each house purchased, he could easily have retired on $100,000 per year or more.

Remember: Many new distributors never realize that only a small success amount of $800 monthly, if invested wisely, can mean financial independence in just a few years. You don't have to be a superstar in network marketing to reach financial security.

Network marketing is so much more than just about us. It is more than just our personal bonus check. It is about how we can **change lives and make a difference**.

Food For Thought

**Thoughts determine
what you want ...**

**Action determines
what you get.**

Think about it.

**Then, share your business and
change people's lives.**

FREE!

GET 7 MINI-REPORTS OF AMAZING, EASY SENTENCES THAT CREATE NEW, HOT PROSPECTS.

Discover how just a **few correct words** can change your network marketing results forever.

Get all seven <u>free</u> Big Al mini-reports, and the <u>free</u> weekly Big Al Report with more recruiting and prospecting tips.

Sign up today at:
<u>http://www.BigAlReport.com</u>

WANT BIG AL TO SPEAK
IN YOUR AREA?

Request a Big Al training event:
http://www.BigAlSeminars.com

Tom "Big Al" Schreiter's books
are available at:
http://www.BigAlBooks.com

See a full line of Big Al products at:
http://www.FortuneNow.com

ABOUT THE AUTHOR

Tom "Big Al" Schreiter has 40+ years experience in network marketing and MLM. As the author of the original "Big Al" training books in the late '70s, he has continued to speak in over 80 countries on using the exact words and phrases to get prospects to open up their minds and say "YES."

His passion is marketing ideas, marketing campaigns, and how to speak to the subconscious mind in simplified, practical ways. He is always looking for case studies of incredible marketing campaigns that give usable lessons.

As the author of numerous audio trainings, Tom is a favorite speaker at company conventions and regional events.

His blog, http://www.BigAlBlog.com , is a regular update of network marketing and MLM business-building ideas.

Anyone can subscribe to his free weekly tips at:

http://www.BigAlReport.com

Printed in Great Britain
by Amazon